Dedication

*This book is dedicated
to the love of my life, my sweet husband Mike...*

*Who has opened my heart to love
and my soul to dreaming without limitation.*

*May you and our beautiful children
always know that you are my most
precious gift...*

*"In healing ourselves we become
the wives and mothers,
sisters and brothers...
that we all deserve
to have and love"*

The importance of making spirituality a part of your daily life is absolutely essential to the healing process. It is only through connecting with our inner selves that we can bring forth the issues in each of us that needs to be healed. Once you begin healing past traumas your aura will take on a vibrant healthy glow and you will experience improved physical energy, greater love and tolerance within your personal relations. You will begin to feel empowered and renewed as you take responsibility for healing the course of your future. If you are dedicated in following the powerful healing techniques outlined in this book, spirituality and self care will become a vital part of your daily life and you will find yourself feeling incomplete without nurturing these aspects within you. The more spiritually fit we become the less it feels like homework and the more it begins to feel like a loving and deserved gift. Get excited about changing your life! Today is the day to begin! Learn to love yourself as you never have before. Remember, without change, nothing changes. You have waited long enough to dance in the sunlight of your spirit!

Heal *your* Aura

Change *your* Life!

IN PRINT PUBLISHING
SEDONA, ARIZONA

© 2005 Jamie Jones

All rights reserved. No part of this book may be reproduced or utilized in any way or by any means, electronic or mechanical, including photocopying or recording, or by an information storage and retrieval system without specific written permission from the publisher.

Published by

In Print Publishing
P.O. Box 20765, Sedona, AZ 86341

Cover Design,
Illustrations and Layout by
Rachel Wyatt
Sedona, Arizona

Jones, Jamie
   Heal Your Aura, Change Your Life!
   LCCN: 2005922376
   ISBN: 1-886966-26-5

Manufactured in the United States of America.

TABLE OF CONTENTS

Foreword vii
Introduction viii

The Importance of the Healing Aura

The History of the Human Aura 1
The Auric Field 3
The Chakra Energy System .4
Spinning and Opening the Chakras 7
The Colors of the Aura 10

The Transformation Begins

Techniques for Healing the Aura 21
Protection While Healing .22
    Grounding Exercise, Auric Bubble Technique
Healing Our Past Traumas 26
Releasing Anger 29
Physical Body Movements to Clear Energy 32
    Base Chakra, Sacral Chakra, Solar Plexus Chakra,
    Heart Chakra, Throat Chakra, Third Eye Chakra,
    Crown Chakra
Maintaining the Health of Your Aura 50
    Salt Baths for Clearing, Power Journaling,
    Sage Wands, Daily Walks, Tarot, Dreams
Strengthening and Healing Your Aura 56
Keeping Your Living Space Sacred 69

☙ AFFIRMATIONS ❧

Foreword...

My work as an aura photographer and spiritual counselor has led me on the most incredible, magical healing journey! Over the past ten years, I have had the privilege of leading seekers from around the world on dolphin swim tours and vortex journeys, as well as photographing and interpreting their auric energy fields. It has been during these trips and counseling sessions that I have witnessed profound life changing moments that can only be described as spiritual miracles. As my clients embarked on a journey of healing their auras, they were awakened to their spiritual gifts and discovered their true life's path for the first time. I witnessed as these seekers, determined to heal their past, changed their lives dramatically by following powerful healing techniques which will be outlined in this book. As a direct result of their efforts they experienced improved health, increased intuition, healthier relationships and a sense of soul empowerment that forever changed their lives. As more individuals hungry for healing and self awareness prepare to take the next step towards this awakening I have heard the same questions voiced time and time again. "How can I heal myself and find inner peace?" "How do I develop my psychic abilities?" "How do I release the past?"

"How do I uncover my potential and live the life I was meant to?" In reading this book, you will learn how to heal your aura and change your life. I will provide you with simple and effective tools to heal your past, increase your intuition, connect with your spirit guides and your higher self to establish a spiritual connection in your life that fulfills you. You have already taken the first step towards changing your life in seeking out this book. Be gentle with yourself and patient with your progress as you heal and transform. By the end of this journey you will have given yourself the magical gift of healing that will forever change the course of your life!

Introduction

For years people have assumed that only gifted and spiritually evolved mediums possessed the ability to be psychic. The truth is that *anyone* can increase their intuition and become more psychic through healing and self awareness. Becoming psychic is a skill that can be learned by anyone with the desire. Through healing our past and clearing our energy blockages, we can more fully develop our intuition and establish a strong connection with our higher selves. Whether your desire is to become a channel who performs psychic readings for others or you simply wish to heal your past and find inner peace and a connection to your angels, the healing techniques in this book can get you on the path to discovering your spiritual potential. I am going to guide you through powerful exercises that will physically clear your auric field and open your chakras enabling you to improve your mental, spiritual and emotional health. As you embark on this incredible journey be aware this healing experience will absolutely change your life! You will forever abandon the role of the victim and reclaim your true soul power! Your dreams and desires will absolutely become a reality if you are thorough in doing this transformational work!

The History of the Human Aura

As early as the 1960s, scientists were beginning to capture the human energy field encircling the human body through a process known as Kirlian Photography. Many of the discoveries in science today recognize we are much more than just our physical bodies, however, it is in the nontraditional arena of psychics and healers that we gain most of our accurate knowledge in the study and understanding of the human aura.

The human body is pulsating with energy and life force. Each cell within our body is moving and changing, flowing with this energy. This energy within the body radiates out creating a circular field around our physical body known as the human aura. The aura can be used as a blueprint for assessing our physical health—identifying our talents and abilities to gain a greater spiritual awareness of ourselves and others. Before we can truly begin to actualize our spiritual potential we must heal certain aspects of our auric field. The unseen energy centers within our bodies, known as the chakras, are also related to the aura and are an integral part of the healing process.

The purpose of this book is to give you greater knowledge in both of these areas so that you may heal yourself and experience greater self awareness and increased spiritual growth. In order to actualize our spiritual potential we must clear our blockages and become willing to fully engage in the healing process.

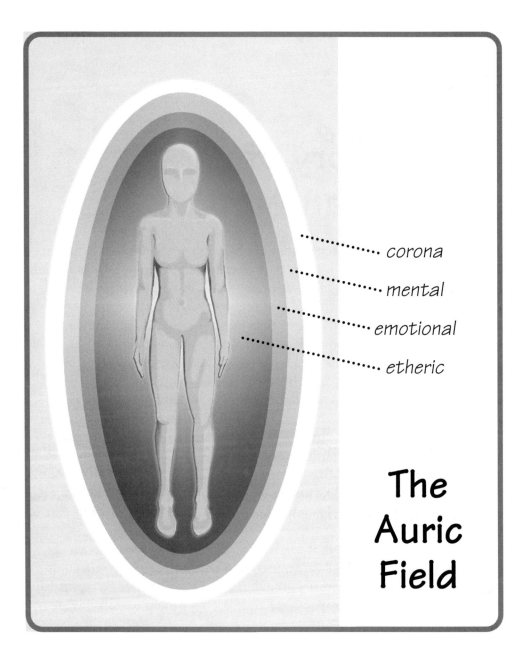

The Auric Field

The auric field is divided into layers of energy that correspond to different levels of your being. Some psychics and healers are able to see and feel each of these energy fields, though it is more common to see only the first three layers of energy around the body.

- The first layer of energy, which lies closest to your physical body is the etheric body. This etheric layer reflects what is happening in the physical body.

- The second layer is the emotional body which can tell us about the individual's current emotional state. It is important to also look to the heart chakra to gain more insight into this area as most traumas and emotional triggers will be stored here.

- The third layer is the mental body which represents our mental activity and ego. It is not uncommon to see blockages in this area that directly affect one's ability to channel and hear their higher selves.

- The fourth layer of the aura is known as the corona and represents the gifts and talents that one has incarnated with from a past life.

These powerful spiritual abilities are just waiting to be awakened and utilized in this lifetime. For most of us this auric field is invisible to the naked eye. However, many of us possessed the ability to see the aura as children and can relearn this technique through practice and training.

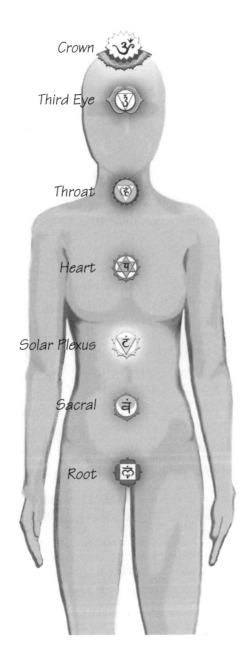

The Chakra Energy System

    The energy flow of the auric field is directly affected by our chakra system. Before we begin the process of healing the aura we must first explore the chakra system in further detail.

    The chakras are the seven main energy centers within the human body system that make up your aura. Each layer of the human aura is associated with a specific chakra. Therefore, keeping the chakras healthy and open will improve your physical and spiritual health which will, in turn, enhance your aura.
I will begin by describing the chakras and their location and finish by explaining how to use visualization and movement to keep the chakras and the aura functioning at their highest level.

* The first layer of the aura and the first chakra, known as the Root Chakra, is responsible for physical functioning and safety/security needs. This base chakra is vital in maintaining life force energy flow to all the other chakras as well as keeping you grounded.

* The second layer and second chakra, known as the Sacral Chakra is associated with the emotional center of the body. Emotional health, sexuality and creativity stems from this center.

* The third layer and chakra, the Solar Plexus, is your power center. The health of this chakra contributes to your self-esteem and confidence and is responsible for how you present yourself to the outside world.

* The fourth level and chakra, the Heart Chakra, is the vehicle through which we give and receive love. This essential chakra affects how we love all others.

❋ The fifth layer and chakra is the Throat Chakra, which is responsible for communication, boundaries with others and empowerment of self.

❋ The sixth chakra and layer of the aura is the Third Eye. This chakra is your intuition and higher self.

❋ The final chakra and the seventh layer is the Crown Chakra. The crown connects you to the higher universal plane of knowledge and to your angels and spirit guides. The chakras are specific locations within our energy systems that are responsible for sensations, thoughts, memories, emotions, and spiritual experiences that we all have. We must keep this entire energy system in balance if we are to achieve our maximum intuitive potential.

Spinning and Opening the Chakras

Now that we have revealed the vital role the chakras play in the overall health of our auras I am going to guide you in a brief exercise that should be performed at least twice a week for the first four weeks and once a week after that period. This exercise is a quick and effective tool in opening the chakras and maintaining a balanced energy flow throughout your entire system. Later in the book I will be guiding you through a more intense series of physical chakra healings and trauma release work, but for now we simply want to begin to set our energy in motion in preparation for the next phase of healing.

I recommend finding a comfortable and quiet place to lie down, although this visualization can be performed sitting at your desk or outside in nature. We are going to begin with the first chakra, the root chakra, and work our way up one energy center at a time until we reach the crown chakra. You will want to read through this entire exercise a couple of times to learn the techniques and then you may close your eyes to execute it properly.

> *Close your eyes and begin to slowly quiet your mind. If extraneous thought forms arise, as they invariably will, simply acknowledge these thoughts and allow them to drift effortlessly out of your mind.*

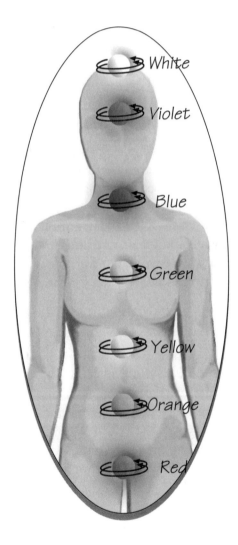

We are going to start with the root chakra located at the base of your spine. I would like you to visualize a golf ball size red light spinning slowly at the bottom of your spine. Gradually imagine this glowing ball of warm red light increasing in size and brightness.

Keep spinning this ball of light in your mind as it increases to the size of a tennis ball. Now hold this image of the glowing ball in your mind while you count slowly to twenty, inhaling and exhaling in long deep breaths…

Simple! You have just activated the energy and performed a clearing of your first chakra and we are now ready to move on to the second chakra, the sacral chakra. We are going to perform the exact same visualization that we just did for the root chakra. I would like you to use the same deep breathing and the same count of twenty. Instead of a red ball of light we are going to use a brilliant orange sphere that also slowly increases in size and intensity. When finished, take a few seconds to clear your mind and relax before moving on to the third chakra, the solar plexus. For this chakra you will be using a yellow ball of glowing sunlight. The heart chakra will follow with the same breathing and counting up to twenty using a green ball of light. We will use blue light for the throat chakra and violet for the third eye. I would like you to finish this chakra spinning exercise with the crown chakra visualizing a sphere of white light at the top of your head. Please refer to the chakra diagram on page eight for the colors that are associated with each chakra for this exercise.

Congratulations! You have just taken one of the most important steps toward healing! The last four weeks of implementing the chakra opening exercise has allowed you to become more aware of your energy centers and to begin to identify issues and blockages that may have been impeding your spiritual healing and progression forward. You may have begun to sense feelings of sadness, pain or fear slowly beginning to surface. Do not panic! This is absolutely normal and crucial to the healing process. This also means that you performed the spinning exercise perfectly! Now we are ready to physically begin releasing the blocks and dissolving the traumas that we have been storing for years. We will now explore the colors of the human aura to give you greater insight into the different energy hues and their meaning. After increasing our understanding of aura energy we will begin the healing transformation in chapter two.

The Colors of the Aura

The human aura is an astoundingly accurate blueprint of who we are and the capabilities that we possess in this lifetime. By having your aura photographed and viewing your colors, much can be revealed. You may uncover hidden talents and abilities that you did not know you possessed, have your past lives uncovered or discover blockages within your energy system that can easily be cleared, opening you up to endless possibilities and opportunities. In the following interpretations of the aura colors and their meanings you will learn about the energy that each color vibration represents. It is my hope that in providing you with a better understanding of the human aura colors you will be inspired to seek out an aura photographer and discover your own divine aura!

Red

Red is the strongest vibration of physical energy that one can have in their aura. Red is the pure life force energy which holds our vitality, passion, movement and activity levels. Individuals who carry a large surplus of red energy in their auric fields are conduits for universal life force energy and have the ability to transfer this energy to others through hands-on touch. Thus, reds are powerful healers and many will gravitate towards the healing fields. If reds do not choose the path of healing they usually find other ways to channel this creative and powerful energy. Reds are the builders, the writers, the chefs, the designers. They are natural leaders and excel in positions of leadership and management. Due to their strong will, reds do best when they have autonomy and freedom within their work environments. When a red is given too much instruction and structure to follow, they tend to feel stifled and frustrated. On the other hand, when reds are given more room to become the creative force in their own business ventures, they feel stimulated and full of joy and will often flourish. To keep attention and productivity high, red individuals should choose careers that involve multi-tasking and freedom of expression. Individuals with red auras are passionate and vital and will find emotional balance when they have a physical outlet for their intense energy through exercise. Reds will quickly tire of mundane schedules and will need plenty of travel to break the monotony of daily routines. Reds like to be direct and confrontational in relationships and can have difficulty relating with another red due to this sometimes abrasive energy. While reds love sex and expressing their sensuality and passion, they lack patience and are more likely to find someone new rather than spend years working on the same relationship.

Reds will find the most harmony when in a relationship with a partner who is emotionally consistent, independent and able to give praise and attention to their red mate. Reds love to test the boundaries and limits by engaging in adrenaline producing activities such as rock climbing, downhill skiing and sky diving. Wise career choices for reds include movie producers, professional athletes, police officers, construction workers, chefs, hands-on healers, interior decorators or entrepreneurs.

Yellow

Yellows are full of dynamic energy and like to take charge in situations whether in work or recreation. The yellow person is intellectual and logical. Yellows are prone to weigh the pros and cons of every situation in detail before making a decision. They have a great talent for organization and are comfortable performing a myriad of duties and tasks simultaneously. Yellow individuals thrive in careers that require a practical and disciplined mind. They feel most comfortable in leadership positions and in control of their environment. Yellows are extremely persuasive and love to debate. Since most yellows rely solely on their intellect to steer their way through life, their intuitive centers and creativity are usually not fully actualized. Yellows find it hard to relax as they are always worrying about what they have to do tomorrow or what they did yesterday. For this reason, they have a difficult time with meditation and will find guided meditation in shorter time periods to be more effective. Yellow personalities enjoy travel and new scenery, yet they often miss the magic of being present in each moment or the joy of spontaneity since they are usually trying to stick to a schedule even while vacationing. Yellows are fabulous planners and find pleasure in making sure that every detail has been attended to. Perfect career choices for yellows are wedding or event planners, accountants, office managers, CEO of large corporations, computer specialists or programmers, sales persons, dieticians, directors, attorneys, psychiatrists or engineers. Yellows need to make certain that whatever they choose to do in this life, they need to be intellectually challenged.

Turquoise

Turquoise individuals are here to be of service and will only feel completely fulfilled when they are being a voice for someone that cannot be heard, fighting for a cause that they believe in or defending someone they render defenseless. I commonly refer to this color as the 'Mother Theresa' energy. Turquoise individuals typically find fulfillment in occupations such as teaching, healing, ministry or counseling. Even if they wind up managing a bank, they will soon find themselves in the role of the bank counselor. Individuals with this color in their auric field will find themselves wanting to keep the peace at any cost and get caught up in the role of the people pleaser. For this reason, it is inevitable that Turquoise individuals will have to work on their boundaries and self-empowerment at some point in their lives.

Pink

Pink in the aura represents unconditional love and protection. When pink appears in the heart chakra it shows that the individual is in love, involving either a new relationship or a child in their life. Also, when pink appears as a separate sphere of energy in one's auric field it can be a new soul waiting to incarnate. For this reason, women who are about to become pregnant or have just conceived will carry this pink ball of light in their auras. When an individual has gone through a great amount of healing and transformational work in the heart chakra area, pink will often be the color that results, indicating that the person has now entered a level of deeper self love and will be ready to draw in a new romantic relationship if desired. Pink is generally a positive color in the aura though the meaning of this color will vary depending on the shade and location. Pink intermixed with white hues in the aura tells us the individual has a spirit guide with them that is infusing them with love and healing energy while watching over them with protection and light.

If pink is radiating out from the heart it indicates the person is seeking a new love relationship. Pink in the area of the channeling window indicates psychic protection.

Orange

Orange is the color of vitality, creativity and adventure! When orange appears in one's aura it means that they are in a space of divine thought and revelation and it is the perfect time to manifest their dreams. Orange is also the color of adventure and excitement. The presence of orange in one's field represents new desires and inspiration to seek out new opportunities and experiences. Orange is a good indication of a fast paced year ahead filled with change and growth. Orange individuals find that they love to socialize and interact with others as frequently as possible. The person with a large amount of orange in their aura welcomes new challenges and works hard to prove themselves in their career. Orange signifies the presence of an inventive mind and the physical and mental energy to carry out their wonderful ideas. Orange typically appears in the aura for periods of one to two years and will then cycle out, giving the individual time to rest and reflect after such an intense and busy energy cycle. The person with orange in their aura should take advantage of the amazing burst of creativity and energy when it appears in their auric field by diligently doing the footwork required to bring their dreams to fruition.

Green

Green is the color of self healing and new beginnings. When green is present in the aura, it indicates someone receiving healing energy, headed for great change. When the aura is green one may feel confused and ungrounded due to the amount of rapid transformation that is occurring in the energy field. However, this is the color of release and necessary growth and should be viewed as the positive opportunity for rebirth is one's life. If we embrace this change rather than fear it, the growth process will move along quite smoothly. Green is the color of exciting new beginnings! Green cleanses and heals the aura—eliminating heavy energy that is no longer serving us. Once this dense energy is carried out of our auric fields we have room to bring in new friendships, opportunities and joy.

Violet

Purple or Violet represents the energy of the wizard and thus the powerful ability to manifest. When purple is dominant in one's auric field it represents the perfect time for starting creative new ventures. Whether they decide on traveling to another country or starting a new business, this is the time when focus and vision becomes clear and powerful. Violet is also the color of intuition and as a result we will find we are divinely guided during the purple phases of our auric development. New guides and teachers will appear during periods of violet and those involved in channeling or psychic work should engage in meditation and/or automatic writing during this phase. Many magical ideas and visions have been known to be "downloaded" during this time and it would be a shame to miss any life changing messages.

White

White represents the highest vibration of spiritual energy. When white is present in the aura we possess increased channeling abilities and protection from our angels and guides. White energy is transcendent and serves as a 'portal' or window in our energy fields through which we can access higher levels of information and guidance.

Individuals with white auras are also known as crystals and can take on the energy of others due to their innate clairsentience. For this reason, I often refer to them as 'auric chameleons' as they are highly adaptable and able to shift and change their energy to blend in any situation. White auras are extremely sensitive to energy and need to protect and cleanse their energy fields on a daily basis. These amazing channels and light beings are suited for counseling, psychic and healing professions.

Indigo Blue

Indigo Blue represents a wisdom and knowledge from traveling many lifetimes. Indigo's are the old souls and the "sensitives" of today. They possess great psychic ability and are usually quite sensitive emotionally. Indigo's wonderful, empathetic nature makes them the perfect candidates for working with children and animals. Blues also possess the gift of communication and are perfectly suited for careers in counseling, human resources, teaching and public speaking fields. They are wonderful problem solvers and advisors and, if they are not professionally employed in a field that requires those skills, they will find themselves counseling and advising everyone in their circle of family and friends. Indigo blues can be gifted healers as well. As wholistic healers, they tend to use their intuition and communication skills to heal a person in conjunction with a hands on approach. Therefore, blues are truly master healers as they not only administer energy via the hands, they also seek to find the emotional and spiritual root or cause of the physical energy blockage within the body. It is in so doing that the master healer can clear issues on all levels so that the physical manifestation does not have to perpetuate.

Indigo Children

Regarding children with indigo in their auras: In her book, *Indigo Children*, Jan Tober describes such children as spiritually gifted "natural born philosophers who think about the meaning of life and how to save the planet" from the moment they are born. I have worked with many "Indigo children" over the years and have found them to possess extremely high energy and emotional sensitivity. Indigo children are indeed psychic and have enormous reserves of creativity. For this reason they quickly tire of mundane routines and appear to have a short attention span. In school they are often labeled ADD or ADHD (Attention Definition-Hyperactivity Disorder) and put into a special resource classroom before they are even given a chance. These children are in fact gifted and simply need more hands-on, stimulating learning environments and teachers who are properly educated to teach them if we are to ensure their success. It is imperative that anyone who has children or works with children understand more about Indigos and how we can foster and nurture their development. These are the spiritually advanced children of the future and it is up to us to help them uncover and develop the talents within. Doreen Virtue's *Crystal Children* is a wonderful new book that describes crystal children as the new generation that has come to the Earth plane after Indigo children. These children are similar to Indigos—highly psychic and sensitive—but without the emotional extremes. If you have your own children or are involved in the care and teaching of other children, I highly recommend that you read these books.

THE TRANSFORMATION BEGINS...

Techniques for Healing the Aura

As we have been learning, the health and vitality of the energy you store inside of your auric field, including the chakras, is crucial to your psychic development and greatly affects the energy you radiate to the outside world. The auric field also encircles us with protection. For this reason, it is important to keep your personal energy field on a routine maintenance plan. The aura can be affected by personal resentments or traumas and also by negative energy that you may absorb from others. Thus, by periodically cleansing and clearing your energy field you can revitalize your aura bringing you improved health, enhanced psychic powers, emotional serenity and mental clarity. The aura can also be negatively influenced by drugs, medications and alcohol use. These causes take longer to clear and in some cases long-term abuse may take years to repair. Follow me now while I describe specific effective healing techniques for improving the health of your aura. Keep in mind you will be performing these clearing exercises quite frequently in the beginning. Each chakra exercise should be done in order starting with the first chakra, the base chakra. Perform each exercise for period of seven days before moving on to the next chakra. As you advance in your healing process, these exercises can be performed with less frequency. For those of you who are practitioners involved in hands on healing or psychic readings, I would advise using some of these techniques on a daily basis.

Protection While Healing

Before we embark on the powerful healing portion of this journey, we must take the steps necessary to protect and seal our auric fields to avoid any trauma to the body. While it is true that we will be pulling energy blockages and traumas to the surface in order to release them, we will always do so in a manner that is as gentle and nurturing as possible. For most of us we will be experiencing deep feelings of sadness and pain as these emotions are uncovered and brought to the surface to be permanently released. However, we never need to retraumatize our physical, spiritual or emotional bodies to do so. While some feelings are uncomfortable, they are not going to harm us and they must be "felt" in order to be released.

Remind yourself that the feelings arising in the following chapter will not harm you! By allowing these emotions to be recognized and felt, they will lose their power over you and you can finally be free of the heavy energy you have carried for too long. You will need to perform the grounding and protection visualizations every morning for two weeks. If you miss a morning or even a week, simply begin again when you can.

Grounding Exercise

Creating a Grounding Cord: For this exercise you will need to sit in a chair or stand with your back completely straight. Anyone involved in healing or psychic work should perform this visualization before each healing session.

> *Visualize a gold cord running along your spine and down through the bottom of your feet into the center of the Earth.*
>
> *See this same gold cord traveling up from your spine through the base of your neck, up through your crown chakra and into the Universe.*

If you do not resonate with the gold cord technique, you may use this second visualization which is my personal favorite:

> *Imagine your body as a sturdy thick tree trunk. The trunk is massive and steady traveling from the top of your head along your torso and down to your ankles.*
>
> *Next, visualize numerous thick branches growing out of your feet and traveling down into the ground, firmly rooting themselves in the core of the Earth.*

These visualizations can be performed in seconds and are extremely powerful in protecting your energy and keeping you grounded in any situation. Any person involved in healing or psychic work should perform this visualization before each client healing session for optimal results.

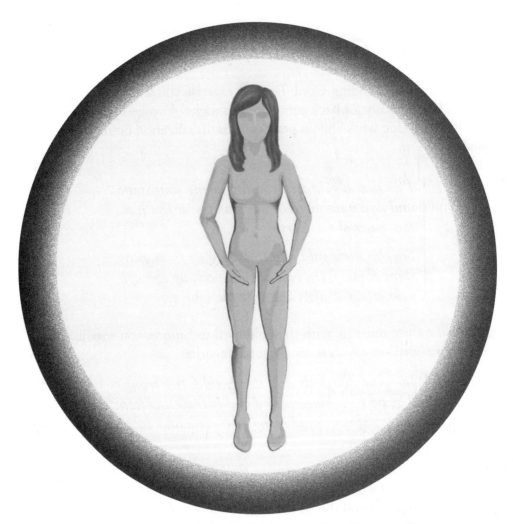

Auric Bubble Technique

Creating an Auric 'Bubble' for daily protection: Your auric field extends arms length out all around your physical body and down into the ground. It is vital to your psychic development that this energy field is kept clear.

> *Standing straight with your arms out in front of you, visualize the space that is your aura. As you do so, do not forget to include the space beneath your feet.*
>
> *Now, imagine this space is surrounded by a brilliant white light. See your body encased in this white bubble and feel yourself surrounded in love and protection.*

If you do not resonate with white, you may choose any other color for this exercise. Be creative and surround yourself in protective and loving shades of pink, purple, green or red!

Once we have practiced the important techniques for grounding, protecting and sealing our auric fields, we are ready to move forward with the deep healing process. In the beginning we are first going to clear our auras of all heavy past traumas and resentments in a series of deep cleansing exercises. This "forgiveness" process is a vital step in clearing our energy fields so that we can create new space within our auric system to bring in new healing energy. Remember, we must release the past in order to move forward. After we have finished the cleansing techniques, I am going to guide you through a series of physical exercises to move out any residual stored energy that has been blocking your vital and healthy energy system. Work at your own pace! You may perform these exercises quickly or perform them weekly with a break or rest in between. Pay attention to your body, noting any changes which may be too sudden or disruptive and take three to five days off to simply rest before returning to the healing techniques and exercises.

Healing Our Past Traumas

Past traumas can negatively impact our energy fields. When we experience a trauma, we tend to hold onto the shame, guilt, fear and anger of what has happened to us for years after the occurrence. These emotions will eventually manifest in our auric fields as blockages and "holes" hindering our ability to move forward in life. In order to move beyond these limitations we must forgive and release the past baggage that we have been carrying. We no longer have to pay the price of hauling this heavy energy around. Upon identifying past events that have been controlling us and limiting our spiritual growth we can release them. Once we truly realize that we create our own realities with every choice that we make and every action we take, we can decide to start creating a new reality by choosing to heal in this very moment. In so doing, we will experience the feelings of true freedom and gratitude knowing we can choose to manifest the lives of our dreams. As you become increasingly conscious and aware you can align with your soul's path and manifest what you desire. The goal is to reclaim our authentic power by releasing the past and to begin creating the future.

The first step in healing our past is forgiving those who we feel may have harmed us. In order to release the toxic emotions associated with our past traumas we need to take our power back. The first step in reclaiming our inner power is to realize we are not victims and we ultimately create every situation in our lives as a learning experience. By owning our part in the forgiveness process we are able to claim responsibility for our lives and release the past. Now I realize that it may be difficult to understand that a three- or four- year old child chose to create a situation where they would be sexually or physically abused. Yet through surviving this experience they have the opportunity to heal and discover within themselves an inner strength and compassion for others that could only be discovered in having to heal and recover from such a trauma. Perhaps their destiny was to experience this so they could go on to heal and counsel others who may encounter this similar trauma. You see, we cannot know what each soul has decided to create as their experience. In this lifetime the truth is *nothing in this universe happens by accident*. We are conscious beings creating our reality in each and every moment.

Remember, on order to heal our past we must first be able to identify our traumas. I strongly recommend buying a journal in which you can list each person or situation that you feel has caused you pain. You may fill the first two pages or the entire notebook. When you are finished, recite the following affirmation and begin to take your power back.

> *"I give you back your shame, anger, and guilt...*
> *They are no longer mine to carry.*
>
> *I realize that you are simply hurting inside*
> *and need help.*
>
> *I release you and all situations which*
> *have caused me harm.*
> *I move forward in love and forgiveness.*
>
> *I am a wonderful, amazing, healthy being*
> *who is taking charge of my life. I am at peace!"*

The idea behind any affirmation is to train your mind to believe what is absolutely true and wonderful about yourself! Repeating this affirmation every day for thirty days is essential to the forgiveness process. You no longer have to listen to the negative tapes, they are simply not true.
The truth is that every one of us is a radiant child of God and we must believe that the power of love and forgiveness resides in us all. When you live in the space of love and compassion, hate and anger simply cannot exist. Pray for those you harbor a resentment for and be amazed as the resentment is replaced with forgiveness. I must also add that some traumatic events from our past may simply be too overwhelming or tragic for us to deal with alone. In these cases where you feel overwhelmed by sadness or grief, I recommend seeking a professional therapist who can guide you through this process of healing. Do whatever it takes to heal yourself, you deserve it!

Releasing Anger

In confronting our past traumas, we undoubtedly have stirred up some anger and resentment… Perfect! Now that we've brought these emotions out in the open, we can release them. Anger becomes a resentment when it is carried for a long time and can be toxic to our bodies. These emotions can cause us to become sick and stuck if we do not work to release them. Anger is a normal emotion that is simply the "lid on the jar of fears" that we have been storing. Remember that FEAR is simply "False Evidence Appearing Real." By confronting the fearful parts of ourselves they lose power over us. As the fear diminishes, the anger that has been hiding the fear will also lessen. As we continue in this process by identifying our part in the situations that triggered the fear and anger, we continue to release these emotions and become FREE!

Physically moving the energy of anger out of your body is a powerful technique that works quickly and effectively. I would like you to choose any of the following methods that feels most comfortable for you. You are going to be screaming quite loudly during these exercises, so you will need to find a safe place to perform this techniques. I call it "growling release" as you will be yelling from deep down in the pit of your stomach. This "scream" will not be coming from your throat, but rather from your diaphragm. Another method is to find a large pillow and scream into it, or you may prefer to roll up the windows of your car and perform this release exercise there. You choose!

> *I would like you to think of a particularly painful incident that caused you to feel shame or anger you would like to release once and for all. This can be a relationship issue, a physical abuse issue, a resentment with a co-worker… anything that you have been harboring a resentment for.*

> *Once you have the issue in mind I would like you to allow the feelings and emotions around the memory to simply come up. As you do so, begin to growl from the depths of your gut. In the beginning of this exercise you may find that you feel like laughing or you may feel like crying. Do not judge yourself for any reaction that you have. Continue growling loudly from your stomach, allowing the anger behind the growl and all emotion to be released and exit your body.*

Remember, these emotions have long been repressed and it will be quite uncomfortable as they begin to surface. However, it is in being persistent with this technique that you will eventually begin to feel a relaxing sensation in the pit of your stomach as this stored anger and fear finally begins to exit your body and then your aura. I recommend performing this technique for a duration of five minutes, three times a week. This energy has been with us for a long time and we do not want to do anything that will be too jarring for the emotional body.

A second powerful release technique is that of prayer. We have all heard of praying for our enemies when practicing forgiveness. And guess what? It really works!

> *Close your eyes for a moment and envision the individual or situation for which you have been storing anger. Slowly begin to imagine this person as a child who has simply been hurt themselves and is only reacting to their own stored pain and anger.*

> *You can now begin to visualize this person surrounded in the brilliant white light of protection while you pray for their highest and best good.*

Naturally, the first few times that you perform this prayer, you probably will not feel like you truly desire the best for this person… but if you are persistent in this exercise, I guarantee that you will eventually feel your anger subside and forgiveness will begin to enter your heart. You are doing this for you—to free yourself of the burden of resentment. Practice this exercise as frequently as you wish, each time knowing that you have given yourself a wonderful gift.

Congratulations! You have just taken one of the most important steps toward healing! The last four weeks of implementing the chakra opening exercise has allowed you to become more aware of your bodies energy centers and to begin to identify issues and blockages that may have been impeding your spiritual healing and progression forward. You may have experienced feelings of sadness, pain or fear slowly beginning to surface. Do not panic! This is absolutely normal and crucial to the healing process. This also means you performed the spinning exercise perfectly! Now you are ready to physically begin releasing the blocks and to dissolve the traumas you have been storing for years.

Physical Body Movements to Clear Energy

Base Chakra

The first chakra we are going to clear is the root or base chakra. This is the chakra where we store all of our safety and security needs. This is also the chakra tied to all of our family issues and where we store most of our fear. In this exercise we will be releasing these fears and reclaiming our power. For this exercise you will need to find a safe space where you can yell or howl without fear of being interrupted of scaring your children!

Stand with your feet shoulder width apart and your arms hanging comfortably at your sides.

Begin by squatting down with your knees extending out over your toes. As you squat, breathe deeply as you count to two on the way down. On the way back up you will also be moving at a rate of two deep breaths. Once you have the squat rhythm down, you will want to begin to visualize a bright red sphere at the base of your spine glowing and sparking in intense red.

Feel the heat of this red sphere as you visualize any black or dark energy you may see being burned up and dissolved by this intense ball of red light. Repeat this exercise until you do not see any more dark energy around your base chakra. Now stand upright in the initial position with feet arms-width apart and begin to howl from your base chakra all the way up your body and out of your mouth. Do not judge the sound of your "howl!" You can scream, shriek, growl or grunt—the purpose is to release the energy! No one is listening to you and you are on a mission. Sound is a very powerful healing tool and the louder you howl and get into it, the better!

Sacral Chakra

The second chakra is the sacral chakra where all of our sexuality and reproductive energy is stored. We are actually going to sit down for this exercise in a cross legged position with our hands in lotus position. Since this chakra is associated with the color orange we are going to use the orange flame to clear this center.

> *Begin by taking three deep breaths in and slowly releasing them. Focus only on your breathing for the next five minutes as you remind yourself that you are safe and protected during this exercise.*

Now visualize a bright orange flame flickering in your sacral center. See this light as glowing and bright and increasing in intensity. As the flame becomes brighter, visualize all dark energy residing there slowly burning up and disappearing.

As you visualize this flame, begin to hum in a monotone vibration. This sound should originate in your sacral center—the center of the flame—and should flow easily and effortlessly up through your throat and out of your mouth. The less exertion during this sound healing, the better, as it should feel warm, easy and soothing to perform.

hmmm...

Solar Plexus Chakra

The solar plexus chakra is yellow in color and is associated with your soul power and your self esteem. Most of us have major blockages in this center since it is directly tied to the ego, and we usually experience profound healing upon clearing this chakra.

Stand with your feet together, back and neck straight and your shoulders pulled back and relaxed. As you get into position, focus on a stance that makes you feel powerful and in charge. Take both of your hands and place them on your sacral chakra with palms facing forward, one on top of the other.

Now visualize the sun—hot and yellow in color—radiating golden rays outward from your solar plexus and filling up the rest of your body. Feel the warmth in your solar plexus begin to flow outward into the other areas of your body, creating a feeling of safety and loving warmth.

As you envision this bright sun, continue to breathe deeply while beginning to make the sound "ah…"

This is the sound of relief and contentment and should flow out of your mouth without the slightest amount of exertion on your part.

Feel the relief and joy of this bright sunlight as you let go of limitation and reclaim the power of your spirit.

After you have executed this exercise for at least five minutes, I would like you to repeat the following affirmation aloud for ten to fifteen times.

"I am manifestation of Light. I stand in my power able to create exactly what I want in my life from this moment on."

Heart Chakra

The fourth chakra, the heart chakra, is the primary energy center of love, emotions and relationships. The heart chakra not only influences how we are able to love others but also how we are able love ourselves.

> *I would like you to lie down on your back with you arms at your side, palms facing up on any comfortable surface. This surface can be a patch of green grass outside in nature, a yoga mat in your home or a bed or couch in your room. The goal is to get into a position that allows your entire body to be supported and to relax so that you are completely able to receive energy freely.*

Your breathing for this exercise should be slow and relaxed, as you normally would breathe when resting. Now close your eyes and begin to imagine someone or something that you love unconditionally. This can be a grandchild, a sister, a pet, a friend… anyone that you feel a great amount of love for.

Next, visualize this person or animal engaged in any fun activity where they are playing and laughing or resting and peaceful. Any scenario that brings a smile to your face as you imagine this person engaged in this activity.

For example, I like to visualize my two-year old son running back and forth through a sprinkler on a hot summer day in the soft green grass. I imagine the details such as his bare feet and sparkling eyes and he dances playfully through the water droplets. Invariably I am smiling and filled with an enormous, overwhelming sense of love, joy and peace.

Your visualization should be something that brings you a similar feeling. Take your time and keep visualizing until that smile falls upon your lips.

Now imagine this person or pet surrounded in bright pink light of unconditional love. This pink bubble or circle of light should encircle them completely and be glowing and bright in color. Feel your heart filling with love as you view the scene before you in your mind's eye.

Next, begin to envision a ray of pink light shooting out from this bubble of love and headed toward you. This "love ray" is all of the love you

> *feel for this other person coming back to you.*
> *As it nears your physical body begin to imagine*
> *this ray of light entering the front of your body*
> *and infusing your heart chakra with the pink*
> *brilliant light of love and joy.*

Be patient with yourself if this ray of light suddenly stops at your body unable to enter your heart. When I first did this exercise, this is precisely what I experienced. I was afraid to let in all of that love, unable to accept that I deserved it. If this is the case for you, I would like you to stop the visualization and repeat the following affirmation ten to fifteen times:

> *I AM love and I deserve to be loved.*
> *I open my heart and receive all of the love*
> *the universe has to offer.*

Once you have done the affirmation, return to the beginning of the exercise and try it again! Patience… patience… the benefits of learning to open the heart chakra to receive love is one of the most powerful healing techniques of all! Once the heart chakra is open to receive love, all blockages will inevitably be dissolved. Keep in mind that this exercise can be repeated as much as you like and should be repeated at least once every couple of months… for the rest of your stay here on earth!

Throat Chakra

The throat chakra is blue in color and directly tied to communication and our ability to relate to others. In my work as an aura photographer, I have found a shockingly high percentage of women in whom this center is closed. In our efforts to please other people and to avoid confrontation or the ruffling of any feathers, many of us have had this chakra blocked for years. Obviously this isn't healthy for our auric health or well being. We need to learn how to open this chakra and discover that stating our boundaries with others and feeling free to speak our truth, will dramatically brighten our auras and increase our spiritual fitness. You will need some writing paper and a pen for this exercise and you may find any comfortable place to sit.

We are first going to visualize a blue swirling vortex of energy in the throat that is increasing in color and size. Breath deeply and concentrate on counting to three as you inhale and three as you exhale.

Relax the muscles in your neck and throat and begin to make an "ohhhh" sound that lightly vibrates up from your diaphragm and glides up through your throat and out of your mouth. The "ohhh" sound should feel cool like a drink of water gliding through your throat area.

Visualize this cool blue water washing away any heavy or stuck energy from your throat. If you feel a lump, or your throat beginning to close, simply acknowledge the resistance and continue with the visualization until it clears.

ohhh...

ohhh...

ohhh...

If you are unable to clear the energy or still feel a slightly heavy or clamping feeling in your throat, discontinue the exercise at this time and retrieve your pen and paper. Try to think of all the situations in which you felt you have not been able to speak your mind or set a necessary boundary with someone. It could be a boss at work or an intrusive family member. Though it may not feel appropriate for you to voice your truth with this person, you can certainly write it out. We are not going to be giving this to the person with whom we have the issue but we are merely going to clear it for ourselves in the privacy of our own home! Now write down exactly what you would like to say, exactly as you would like to say it. After you have written this down, find a mirror somewhere in your house and read this "letter" aloud. In doing this exercise, you are going to be releasing this stored energy once and for all. You may find you have two letters to write or twenty! Remember not to judge yourself but remind yourself that you are getting closer to healing your aura and reaching your total potential! After you have finished the letter writing, return to the first portion of this exercise and visualization and repeat again.

Third Eye Chakra

The third eye is violet in color and is directly tied to our intuitive centers. This sixth chakra is the area of meditation that must be opened if we are to access guidance from our higher selves. Once we are able to open this center we will experience a drastic increase in our psychic abilities and a dissolution of the ego. For this exercise you are going to need an amethyst crystal and a quiet place to meditate.

> *Sitting cross legged with your hands in lotus position on your knees, close your eyes and begin to listen to only the sound of your breathing.*
>
> *As you concentrate solely on your breathing allow all other background noises to slowly quiet— for busy thoughts in your mind to drift away.*

Now pick up the amethyst crystal and place it on your forehead directly on your third eye. Begin to breathe out small puffs of air in succession as you visualize all cloudy and dark energy flowing out from the third eye and evaporating into the air. These short 'labor breaths' should release only tiny clouds of energy at a time.

The amethyst crystal has created the portal or opening in which this blocked energy can be released, however, we must do so slowly.

I would like you to perform this exercise for only five minutes at a time for seven days.

Crown Chakra

The crown chakra is our connection to all higher planes. This glowing white energy center is directly responsible for our connection with our spirit guides and teachers, the angels and to universal knowledge. Once you have performed all of the preceding chakra exercises, you will be able to move ahead with the physical clearing of the crown chakra. For this exercise you will need a clear quartz crystal in any shape or size. The idea is to choose a crystal that "calls" to you, whether it is a new crystal with a rainbow inside that catches your eye or one with sentimental value given to you by a mentor or loved one. This exercise is best performed outside in nature as we will be using the wind and the gentle breezes to clear and activate the crown chakra. If it is raining you may need to wait for a clearing in the weather to execute this final clearing exercise.

Sit directly on the earth with your legs crossed and your hands on your knees, palms facing up.

Place the crystal in front of you on the ground where you can easily see it. I would now like you to close your eyes and focus on the sound of your breathing as you take slow, deep breaths—inhaling through your nose and exhaling through your mouth.

Once you begin to feel your body relax and your mental thoughts begin to quiet, begin to notice the feeling of the wind blowing against you body. If this is a strong breeze you may feel the hair on your arms blowing or your hair sweeping across your forehead. Perhaps there is only a gentle breeze and you can barely feel it dancing on your lips or gliding past your fingertips. Just take note of the feeling of this wind as it effortlessly and easily blows around you.

Now I would like you to focus on the area directly on the top of your head—the crown chakra. Do you feel the wind there? Is it warm from the sun? Maybe this area is already tingling as you begin to focus on the energy there. Do not judge the feeling you have in this area, simply allow it to be.

Imagine the breeze, whether strong or gentle, slowly beginning to open this chakra and blowing away any dark or heavy energy that may be obstructing it.

Visualize a swirl of wind at the top of your head, like a mini tornado, lifting away any "debris" and opening up the top of your head beneath it. This opening in the crown chakra may begin about the size of a quarter and then slowly open up to the size of a saucer.

With your eyes still closed, continue to visualize this energy center being cleaned out by the wind and opened up by the swirl of the breeze.

Finally, I would like you to open your eyes and stare directly at the crystal on the ground in front of you. Once you have the image of the crystal in your mind's eye close your eyes again. Now imagine your face inside the center of this crystal.

Hold the image in your mind of your crown chakra glowing on the top of your head, radiating a brilliant white ray of light. Holding this picture in your mind, continue to envision the image of your face with your radiant crown chakra in the center of your crystal.

The crystal is going to help us to permanently hold the "vision" and the energy of our healthy, open crown chakra once we leave this exercise, so it is important to get a clear image and hold this picture for approximately three full minutes.

When you have completed this portion of the exercise I would like you to become aware of your surroundings again. Feel the earth beneath your legs and begin to notice the sounds of nature around you as you slowly open your eyes and continue to breath.

You have now finished the final physical chakra exercise in this healing series. You'll need to be gentle with yourself as you proceed through your day as you have just performed a major clearing and healing cycle. Remember, you may return to any of the chakra exercises at any time that you feel necessary and perform the exercises to reopen or realign yourself.

By now we have begun to implement powerful techniques for healing past traumas and blockages and are beginning to reap the rewards of our healthy renewed auras. We are now ready to shift our focus to maintaining the health of our radiant energy fields to ensure that we can continue to benefit from our healthy auras. Strengthening and refreshing the aura can keep us feeling positive and motivated to keep moving forward in our growth process.

Maintaining the Health of Your Aura

Daily exercise is absolutely essential in maintaining the health of our energy systems. A simple walk around the neighborhood, breathing in the fresh air can suffice. Running on the beach taking in the sights and sounds around you will keep your chakras clear and your aura vibrant. Another fabulous form of exercise that incorporates your spiritual health is Yoga.

This popular form of exercise is a phenomenal tool for centering and balancing our intuitive, physical and emotional bodies. By moving the energy within our bodies through yoga, we can release deep emotional traumas which have stored in our bodies on a cellular level. When traumas are released, our bodies' vibrations raise allowing us to become clearer channels and lightworkers. Once mastered, the repetition of specific yoga positions and exercises allows the conscious mind to quiet while the subconscious is free to explore higher realms. Yoga, therefore, can provide deep healing which will allow us to uncover our psychic selves, providing a gateway to access higher dimensions. Tai Chi, Qi-Gong, martial arts and Dahn exercise are just some of the other spiritual disciplines that exercise our psychic minds. When the energy centers known as the chakras are properly functioning we can expect to experience an increase in our health on all levels.

Silent or guided meditation is essential for keeping our auras clear and balanced.

The following meditation can be performed as often as you would like for a quick and powerful "aura tune-up."

Salt Baths for Clearing

By simply adding sea salt to your nightly bath, you can instantly clear your energy field of negative unwanted energy that you may have absorbed from others. This clearing bath technique should be used as often as you would like but at least twice a week.

Power Journaling

Power journaling is one of the most powerful techniques that you will find for this type of "brain dump." I call it brain dump since that is exactly what we are doing—we are taking out the mental trash where fear, limitation and stress reside and dumping it out so our inner voice—our intuition—can be heard with greater clarity. In the exercise that follows, I will ask you to write two to three pages every morning in a notebook of your choice. This writing should consist of whatever is on your mind in that moment. Perhaps it is the dreary weather on that particular day, or the upcoming presentation you have to make at work, or the fight you had with your spouse last night. Whatever the subject matter, you are not to grade or judge yourself. The writing is only yours to see and does not have to be written for anyone other than yourself. This journaling does not have to contain life changing, profound revelations—although it may at a later date—it simply gets to be about anything. Just let the ink flow from your pen. After you have been practicing this for some time you will find the information becomes much more profound and may even begin to hold messages from your guides. This is due to the fact that you have cleared out the clutter and you are now an open channel. Do have patience for the first 30 days and practice this technique religiously. You will be amazed before you are half way through.

In her book, *The Artists Way*, Julia Cameron refers to this technique as "morning pages." What sounds like a simple journaling exercise is easily one of the most powerful tools in the actualization of your spirit self. I will call this technique "power journaling," as it not only increases your intuition but also provides deep levels of healing and clearing in one's life. When writing on a regular basis we are able to access and bring to the surface emotional traumas and wounds from the past allowing us to finally release emotions which have been repressed and buried. It is important that you commit to writing on a daily basis for a period of at least 30 days.

> *I am going to ask you to write two full notebook pages every morning when you first wake up. You are to write about anything that is on your mind at that point in time. We are not going to judge our journaling or worry about spelling and grammar. You are going to pick up the pen let it all flow.*

When you are finished, put the journal away and do not open it again until the next morning. If you do miss a day or skip a week to go on vacation, do not reprimand yourself. Simply pick up the next day or the following week and begin again. Remember, power journaling is a wonderful spiritual gift to yourself, not a homework assignment. Have fun and be prepared to discover a new you!

Sage Wands

Native Americans have long practiced the ritual of purifying their energy fields and the energy of particular locations using sage. Sage wands are an easy and effective tool for quickly cleansing one's auric energy field and can be found in most health food stores or new age shops. Sage can also be burned in loose form in any type of fire safe bowl or shell. The smoke from the sage will rapidly clear the energy of any home or work space. Healing practitioners and psychic readers should always use sage to cleanse their work environments following a client session. If you do not prefer the smoke that invariably accompanies the use of sage, you may use the salt baths or burn clearing candles to achieve the same effect.

Daily Walks

Aside from the obvious physical health benefits of the daily walk, the mental and emotional clarity that one achieves is far greater. The fresh air and the sounds of nature will inspire and refresh any spirit! Each and every walk can be a mini vacation if you allow your mind to take you there! If it happens to be a sunny day and you have chosen a scenic route, allow yourself to pay attention to the flowers and the delightful chirping birds along your path. Feel the glowing rays of the sun warming your face while the gentle breeze caresses your cheeks. As you walk and your blood flow increases, deeply breath in the fresh air and simply relax in the pure perfection of the day. Allow all stress and tension to slip away knowing that you do not have to worry about what has to be done the rest of the day during this walk. This is your time to nourish yourself-physically, emotionally and spiritually. If it happens to be a rainy day with cloudy skies, your mini vacation can be just as magical! Bundle up in your rain slicker and boots and head out into the moist air. Allow the sound of the rain hitting the Earth to cleanse your soul. Rather than trying to stay dry, look up into the sky and allow the water droplets to tickle and bathe your face. Breathe in the amazing smell of the new rain and all the scents that the rain brings to life. Kick and splash in the puddles along your path and allow the child in you to play… play… play! You will return home feeling refreshed and rejuvenated!

Tarot

Tarot is a great tool for practicing and perfecting your intuitive abilities. A great tarot deck for the beginner is the *Rider Waite* deck and book set. This deck features the major arcana and includes a book that will explain the cards and their meanings, as well as provide you with sample layouts and reading types. Once you are familiar with the major arcana it will be easy for you to move on to other tarot decks. In the beginning you may rely on the book to give you the meanings or readings of the cards, however it is important for you to put the book away after some time and practice just looking at the images on the cards and see what you intuitively feel or sense from them. For example, the book may define the Tower card as symbolizing change or separation, the death of a relationship. But you may also feel that it is the beginning of something new and a necessary change in one's life so they can move forward in a new direction. Do not be afraid to ask your guides to assist you in the reading and to voice any additional messages that you may receive. At first your mind may tell you you might be "wrong" and look stupid if the information is wrong. In this case, acknowledge the voice of limitation and then proceed to voice the information anyway. The more you trust your gift and share your message, the more you begin to open up to your higher guidance. We must release the blockage in our minds that is fear generated and move forward in trust. Trusting your intuitive voice will always be a struggle in the beginning. With practice this voice will become louder and we will realize that it has been there all along and is as natural as breathing.

Dreams

Dreams can hold powerful and amazing revelations about our past, present and future. Not all of us remember our dreams every morning but as we do the work to increase our psychic abilities, our dream states usually awaken as well. By learning how to interpret our dreams we can gather amazing insight into our futures and obtain messages from our spirit guides and teachers. At the end of your 30-day program, or perhaps sooner, you may discover that your dreams become increasingly vivid and lucid. You may choose to find a psychic that can aid you in interpreting your dreams though I strongly recommend that you learn to interpret your own. Remember dreams are personal and unique to each individual so what a snake symbolizes for one person may be entirely different for another. To ensure the most accurate interpretation, you may gather ideas or insights from others but ultimately you will have to decide if those meanings are accurate representations for you.

To begin interpreting your dreams you may want to purchase a dream notebook to keep a log on the dreams you can remember. Of course it is best to record these dreams as soon as possible. If you awaken during the night after an extremely powerful dream, you should record this in your journal immediately while you still have the clarity of the dream. If you are not able to record your dream until morning, just be sure to jot down as many details as possible, including any symbols or diagrams you may not be able to explain with words. Next to these words and symbols begin to write down what these represent or mean to you. Sometimes this will include a brief description of feelings or events that were triggered and other times it will be only one word. Do not analyze this too much at this point. Just write whatever comes to mind.

Strengthening and Healing Your Aura

Our energy fields may be adversely affected by environmental factors such as pollution and radiation. Living in an environment where we can breath the fresh ocean air or the oxygen rich landscape of nature will be positively cleansing to the energy of our auras and our chakras. By keeping our energy systems clear we are able to heal more rapidly and maintain clarity in our intuitive centers. Maintaining our physical health is imperative to our spiritual well being.

Exercise is an integral part of strengthening and balancing the aura. As we have already discussed, yoga, is an amazing form of exercise which aligns and clears the chakras as well as activating our psychic centers. However, dancing is also a fabulous form of exercise which will increase circulation, reduce stress and increase chakra health. All of which are directly responsible for increasing our psychic abilities.

Relaxation and creativity are two important elements in activating our psychic selves. By decreasing our stress levels we will drastically reduce any blockages in our energy systems and our psychic channels will open up enormously. This includes getting enough sleep at night and devoting at least 20-30 minutes a day in activities that you enjoy and find relaxing. When we are at the height of creativity, we are also most intuitively open. Therefore, engaging in fun and creative projects will not only relax us but access and exercise the right side of the brain where our intuition also resides.

BEFORE

AFTER

Crown Chakra

Opening Exercise

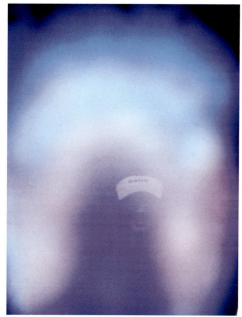

The white represents the highest spiritual vibration of energy which means this person is open to channel and possesses psychic abilities.

Third Eye & Crown Chakra
Clearing Exercise

BEFORE
This individual is a powerful teacher and healer, yet the intuitive and creative energies in her field are not as powerful or vibrant as they could be.

AFTER
After running energy into third eye and crown centers we see a dramatic increase in violet and white energy which represents her creativity and intuition. This is her higher potential energy simply being reactivated.

Throat Chakra
Clearing Exercise

BEFORE
Before Throat Chakra exercise the throat chakra is cloudy and area is closed down. The individual is not speaking her truth or setting clear boundaries.

AFTER
After Throat Chakra exercise note the red life force energy at the throat, signifying that this chakra is now open and the individual is speaking her truth and empowered.

Heart Chakra
Opening Exercise

BEFORE

AFTER

After Heart Opening Chakra exercise heart is full of red life force and has opened dramatically. Also—white "window" shows that she is open to her angels again.

Third Eye Chakra
Opening Exercise

AFTER

After —note the intense violet/blue and white energy moving in at the right indicating an increase in spiritual and intuitive energies.

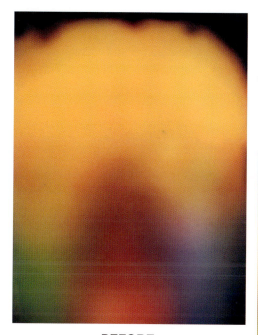

BEFORE

Before Third Eye Chakra opening exercise this individual is spiritually blocked due to heavy mental activity and stress.

Complete Chakra Healing

BEFORE

The muddy yellow-green energy represents mental and emotional blockages of stress, worry and fear. The individual is in dire need of emotional clearing as indicated by the green in the heart chakra. Her mind is in a space of fear and doubt, and the ego is dominant and producing limitation. We can see the blue on the side, representing trust and harmony. However, this energy will not advance into the aura until we can clear the yellow-green blockages.

AFTER

After completing the series of physical chakra healings, this individual has a healthy, balanced aura. She has been empowered and is surrounded in peace and joy. The white arch over her head shows she is out of the ego and in alignment once again with her intuition and higher self.

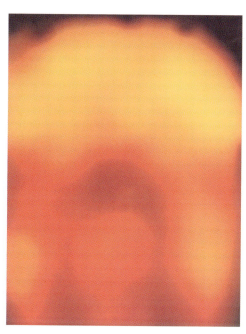

This is an example of an individual with powerful red healing energy and a great amount of mental activity. This person does well in positions of advisement, mentoring and leadership. They prefer to be in control of situations and require a great degree of intellectual stimulation as they are left-brain dominant.

This individual is in a phase of great self-healing and transformation. The red on the left side of the picture represents the letting go of a stressful situation—in this case a stressful job—and the healing green energy occurs as a result. The burst of turquoise on the right side represents more peace and harmony within herself and her environment as a result of the stress leaving.

This is an example of someone who is a great counselor and teacher. She enjoys leadership and prefers to communicate her needs and desires up front. This individual is here on the earth plane to learn through her human relationships.

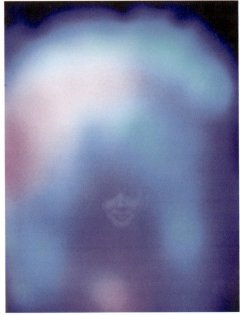

White in the upper left corner represents an opening to channel. When present white reveals that the individual is tapping into higher energies such as spirit guides and universal knowledge to help others. This is the photo of a psychic reader and healer. The pink represents protection coming from her angels.

*Before alignment with soul's path.
A period of healing and transformation.*

After clearing and aligning with path, white shows higher spiritual connection to guides. Heart is full and open.

Before transition and healing period. Confusion, lacking clarity, but a powerful teacher and healer. Simply needs cleansing and emotional healing.

After healing and clearing the individual is clear and in his power working as a teacher and healer. White represents he is channeling and protected by his guides.

Couple

The similar indigo outer layer of both auras represents a couple that has shared a past life together. The large amount of white signifies a great spiritual connection where the couple is in harmony on all levels. The turquoise represents friendship and communication between the individuals.

His photo contains a majority of violet which signifies great creativity and passion.

Jamie

Mike

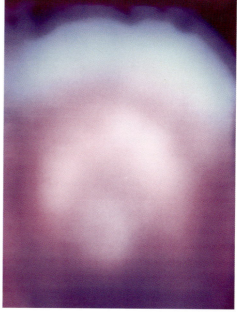

Her photo is mainly blue with shades of fuschia pink representing great vision, speaking skill and desire to be of service to others.

This couple is an ideal match energetically and could do great working together and aligning career paths.

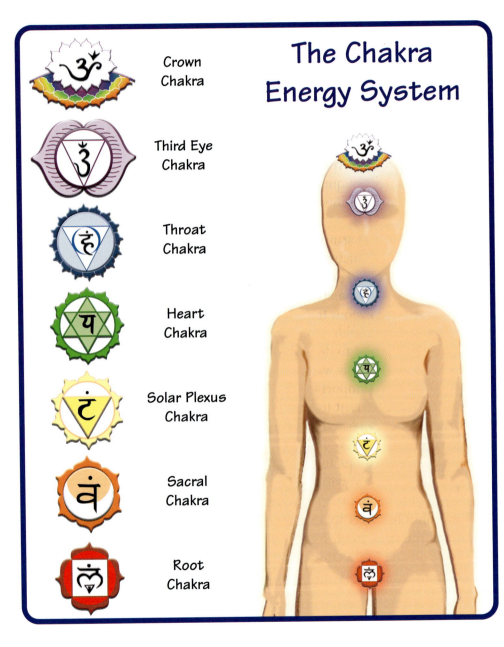

Keeping Your Living Space Sacred

Feng Shui has recently increased in popularity and many have discovered the impact of the energy in which you surround yourself to your state of mind and well being. Feng Shui is the art of placement of objects within our environments that promote harmony and clarity. Once our external spaces are harmonized we find a peaceful internal environment is easier to maintain. You may choose to learn more about the art of Feng Shui though the techniques for clearing listed below are based on the fundamentals of Feng Shui and will provide you with quick and easy results.

The first step in harmonizing an environment is to clear the space of any clutter. Begin reducing the litter by throwing away anything that is no longer needed. Hanging on to old stuff will only weigh your energy down. If you have not used something in three years you probably have no use for it. We cannot make room for positive energy in our lives until we are willing to release the old.

You will also want to do some light cleaning at this time. Dusting and washing the windows, as well as washing anything that has long been neglected will be an important part of this step.

Finally, you will want to add some items to your space that will enhance the energy flow and raise the vibration. Fountains can be added to any room to increase the flow and ease within your environment both internally and externally. Round picture frames, replacing square ones, will promote wholeness and oneness within your relationships. Live green plants will increase the life force energy throughout the home.

Feng Shui has recently increased in popularity and many have discovered the relation of the energy in which you surround yourself to your state of mind and well being. Feng Shui is the art of placement of objects within our environments.

Affirmations

Affirmations are amazing and loving ways to replace negative thought with positive ones. In doing so, you will change the course of your life. Beneath each affirmation on the following pages write down six more affirmations that are loving and true of yourself.

"I am a healthy radiant light being, free of all attachments and aversions to unnecessary distractions in my life."

_____
_____
_____
_____
_____
_____
_____
_____
_____
_____
_____
_____
_____
_____
_____
_____
_____
_____

Affirmations

"Life is a fabulous adventure and I move forward in gratitude and forgiveness today."

Affirmations

"I am in perfect alignment with God's will for my life."

Affirmations

*"I choose to create prosperity and joy in my life.
I am an abundance magnet."*

_____
_____
_____
_____
_____
_____
_____
_____
_____
_____
_____
_____
_____
_____
_____
_____
_____
_____
_____
_____

Affirmations

"I develop my psychic abilities with ease. I trust my inner voice and release all fear as I do so."

Affirmations

"Each and every day presents the wonderful opportunity to learn and grow."

Affirmations

"I radiate love and light to those around me and I attract supportive and loving people in my life."

Affirmations

"The power to heal and transform is within me. I dance now in the sunlight of my spirit."

Affirmations

"I am full of vibrant and healthy life force energy now."

Affirmations

"I love and appreciate myself... exactly as I am!"

Affirmations

"Each and every day, I let my excitement about life lead me toward following my path and actualizing my dreams. I am inspired in each moment to share my joy and spiritual discoveries with others."

Raising Psychic Children

Indigo Children: In her book, *Indigo Children*, Jan Tober describes Indigo children as spiritually gifted "natural born philosophers who think about the meaning of life and how to save the planet" from the moment they are born. I have worked with many Indigo children over the years and have found them to also possess extremely high energy and emotional sensitivity. Indigo children are indeed psychic and possess enormous reserves of creativity. For this reason they get bored quite easily with mundane routines and appear to have a short attention span. In school they are often labeled ADD or ADHD (attention definition-hyperactivity disorder) and put into a special resource classroom before they are even given a chance. These children are in fact gifted and simply need a more hands-on, stimulating learning environment and teachers who are properly educated to teach them if we are to ensure their success. In my next book *Raising Psychic Children*, I'll explain how we can create discovery-rich environments for our children which promote hands-on learning and aids them in staying on task. I'll also discuss the importance of diet and exercise, making choices on their own, structured schedules and supplemental home schooling to ensure the future success and enlightenment of our children. It is imperative that anyone who has children or works with children understand more about Indigos and how we can foster their development. These are the spiritually advanced children of the future and it is up to us to help them uncover and develop the talents within. Doreen Virtue's *Crystal Children* is a wonderful new book that describes crystal children as the new generation that has come to the Earth plane after Indigo children. These children are similar to Indigos—highly psychic and sensitive—but without the emotional extremes. If you have your own children or are involved in the care and teaching of other children, I highly recommend my next book.

About the Author

Jamie Jones, with a BS in Education, has worked as an inspirational speaker, spiritual teacher, author and aura photographer for the past ten years. She has used biofeedback imaging to photograph and interpret the human energy fields of thousands, assisting them in healing and actualizing their spiritual potential. In doing this work, Jamie has gained national recognition and has appeared on ABC's *Good Morning America* and *The Bachelorette*, PBS, TLC and various other TV and radio shows. Jamie is the author of *Sedona's Best Vortex Guidebook* and has guided clients to these magical vortex sites to capture their healing transformations on film.

The owner of Aura Essence Aura Photography, Jamie utilizes her unique blend of intuition and spiritual knowledge to assist others in discovering and living the life of their dreams. With aura photography store locations in Scottsdale, Sedona and Phoenix, Jamie is available for private aura readings and consultations. Aura Essence Aura Photography is also available for group events, business conferences and private parties, all of which can be booked through her website at: www.auraessence.com.